Listen to These Pictures

Listen to These Pictures

Photographs of John Lennon
by Bob Gruen

Text by Bob Gruen and Stanley Mieses
Designed by Bob Gruen and Nick Egan
Foreword by Yoko Ono

WILLIAM MORROW AND COMPANY | NEW YORK

I THANK ALL THE PEOPLE
WHO HAVE HELPED ME MAKE THIS BOOK—
WITH SPECIAL THANKS TO YOKO ONO,
KARLA MERRIFIELD, VIRGINIA LOHLE,
STANLEY MIESES, NICK EGAN, RICHARD ROBINSON,
TOM WINER, BOB MARKEL,
JEAN CAMPBELL, NADYA, KRIS,
AND MY FAMILY.

Grateful acknowledgment is made for permission to reprint lyrics
from "I Can Help" by Billy Swan. Copyright © 1974.
Combine Music Corp. Used by permission. All rights reserved.
International copyright secured.

Library of Congress Cataloging in Publication Data

Gruen, Bob.
  Listen to these pictures.

  1. Lennon, John, 1940–1980—Portraits, etc.
I. Mieses, Stanley.   II. Title.
ML420.L38G78   1985   779'.23'0924   84-22763
ISBN 0-688-04707-6

Printed in the United States of America

First Edition

1 2 3 4 5 6 7 8 9

A portion of the profits of this book will be donated to The Spirit Foundation.

THE WAY WE WERE

Both John and I carried a definite aversion to unkind aggressive photographers for reasons you might guess. Bob was always considerate without
overtly flaunting his kindness. It was nice. In the beginning we thought
maybe he was just that way - quiet. Later we found out that he was quite
a talker himself - like us. So we hit it off on a human level. I think
the way he was had a great deal to do with how we looked in his pictures -
relaxed. Sometimes you see pictures of us looking angry and you draw the
conclusion that the anger was our statement towards the world confusion
or something, when actually it was just us getting nervous with a rude
photographer: vibes of the cameraperson affecting the subject, etc.

I went through the pages of this book and started to hear the song "The
Way We Were." The film was a big hit in the mid-seventies and the theme
song became "our song" for John and Yoko. I still think it was a bit
strange that with all the songs we wrote between us the song we called
"our song" was by Marvin Hamlisch, but that's how it was - and how we
were: just being us and enjoying it.

love,

Yoko Ono
N.Y.C. July 18th '84

This Book is Dedicated to Mother & Child

Introduction

The question I've been asked most consistently for the past ten years is without a doubt "What was John Lennon really like?" Whenever the question was posed it always seemed to imply that John was in some way different from the public's perception of him, and that as his personal photographer I was able to see him in a light that revealed "what he was really like." Without dismissing the question totally, my initial and constant response has been to say that only Yoko can answer that question with the sort of details the inquirer would find satisfactory.

Anyone else's comments must contain a qualification. Mine: I know what John Lennon was like as far as my eyes could see, and I have been able to share much of that with the aid of my cameras. I was in the very fortunate position of seeing quite a bit of John Lennon while he lived in New York, and our relationship was both professional and friendly. He was my favorite subject and he was a mate, in the British sense of the word. As we became friends, it developed that John often came to our meetings without the cynical pop star attitude, and likewise, I arrived without my cameras. I'm proud of the pictures I took of him, but I'm also proud of the pictures I didn't take. I've never been a paparazzo. I respected the difference between the public persona and the private man. There are times when you can allow private moments to be public—this is why a celebrated personality of the magnitude of a John Lennon would require the services of a personal photographer. It was an advantage in my position to be friends with John and Yoko because it meant never having to respond to a formal request; I always heard, "Bring your cameras *if you like.*" And it happens to be my particular edge as a photographer to sense the optimal time to use my camera in a situation where others might be perceived as disruptive. John and Yoko felt comfortable with me from the start, and in a variety of situations where I was the only attendant "nonfamily" person, my presence was never regarded as an intrusion. This allowed me to view many private moments over the years—moments that I did not document but that informed my choices when I did take photographs.

If I had to split it down the middle, I'd say I took pictures of John and I worked with Yoko. Of course, I photographed the two of them, because in all the time I knew them they were virtually inseparable. But any business transaction went through Yoko. She made the appointments; I brought the finished prints to *her*. I was not on their staff, but John and Yoko paid all my expenses, which was helpful since they asked for individual prints of all my photographs (not contact sheets, which was the standard way of working) and they wanted to see everything instantly. I got paid by selling the pictures, sometimes to magazines and newspapers, sometimes to the record company for an album cover. An art director for Apple Records, Al Steckler, gave me good advice about working with John and Yoko. He told me, "John and Yoko will want all kinds of unusual things. They're artists and they think up projects and they hire people to make these projects a reality. You'll often have to figure out how to make something you've never made before—and they'll want it within ten minutes of when they thought of it. Just remember: It's more important to do it right than to do it immediately." I followed that advice. I believe that because they knew me and trusted me, their impatience to see the finished job was mitigated, and because I felt a responsibility as the person they called on, they had confidence the job would turn out right. In time, this became a given between us, and therefore I was privy to a number of exceptional circumstances.

Addressing the question posed to me countless times, I can say that John Lennon was a remarkable and singular creative artist and human being. I have been photographing rock stars since before the genre of rock photography came into being, and I have been in the presence of many, many personalities on the scene who have granted me access to whatever I wished—yet only John (and Yoko) consistently excited me, challenged me, entertained me, educated me, and just plain kept me going. I was always impressed by the dynamic balance of their relationship and the strength it held for both of them. John was clever, curious, intense, quick with an idea and quicker still with a witty response. He was amazingly perceptive of people's situations and their predilections and his intelligence was constantly refreshing.

So was his unpretentiousness and inbred humility, a side of him that grew stronger in his years offstage and off camera. And where John couldn't, Yoko could. She has a marvelous talent for organization, and a confidence in business that stems from a vision of what she wants, not from the power of being a millionaire. I like to think that she protected him and took care of him and that through his life and his music he took care of the rest of us.

Part One

The first time I saw John Lennon was in the fall of 1971. He was standing with Yoko backstage at the Apollo Theatre in Harlem where he had performed at a benefit for the Attica prisoners. A lot of people were circulating around them, snapping pictures. I remember John saying, "What happens to all these pictures? We never see them." I asked him, "Do you really want to see mine? I live right around the corner from you." He said, "Slip them under the door then." And I did.

I was formally introduced a few weeks later, the result of my being interviewed for a book about rock photographers. The interviewer had an assignment to write a magazine article about the Elephants' Memory Band whose record John and Yoko were producing, and he asked me to come along and take pictures. I was told to meet him and John and Yoko in a hotel uptown; apparently too many people were finding their Greenwich Village apartment convenient. I was waiting in the hotel lobby when the writer came down and told me, "Listen, John and Yoko just woke up, and they weren't expecting a photographer and they feel kind of cranky. But don't worry, because they'll wake up in a few minutes and they'll feel better and they'll let you come up. You'll take great pictures of them and they'll like you and love your pictures. You're going to be great friends with them, and you'll do album covers for them, because that's the way they are." Hard to believe, but that's exactly how it progressed: The session was straightforward, professional, and I took pictures of John and Yoko that night; they liked them, we got to be friends, and it lasted a long time.

After his interview, the writer asked if John and Yoko would consent to a picture at the recording studio with the band. The interview had gone well and although they were cautious about allowing photographers into the studio, somehow I didn't bother them. So I climbed into the back of their station wagon with all the guitars and I packed off to the studio with them. Walking in, I lined up behind John. The band was assembled in the control room, and when John arrived he walked into the studio part and motioned for me to follow him. In the back of the room he held open a door to a small and enclosed singer's booth, and to me he said, "In here." Everyone else was in the control room. John shut the door and cautioned me to keep quiet. Over the intercom, the engineer said, "John, we're ready," and suddenly music came out of the speakers and he started singing—not just singing, *recording*. Maybe thirty seconds passed from the time we got out of the car until he started singing. And what was he singing? "Woman Is the Nigger of the World." It took a few moments for me to comprehend the situation. This was a provocative song, especially for the time, and a far cry from what I expected to hear. I certainly had no idea why I was standing in the vocal booth with him. But my presence in an intimate setting with John was accepted without fanfare. This became the basis of our relationship.

At the end of the night as everyone was ready to leave, I reminded Yoko of our plan to take a picture of the whole group. As always, she organized everyone and they walked back in, sat down on the floor together, and I took a picture. It was relaxed and informal. The Elephants had a somewhat notorious reputation and John liked the idea of a creative association with a New York City street band; there was a genuine camaraderie between them. We went out to Forty-fourth Street in front of the recording studio, and for a while they played their guitars and everyone improvised a song out in the cold and slush.

It never occurred to me thereafter that John and Yoko would want to see my pictures or that I could even contact them; I thought they were much too busy and certainly had photography under control. So I accepted an assignment to make a film for Ike and Tina Turner who were about to embark on a national tour. A few weeks later I came back to New York and ran into Rick Frank from Elephants' Memory. He had been trying to find me because I was the only one who took pictures of the group with John and Yoko in the studio and they needed one for the album cover. Rick wanted to show the pictures to John and Yoko the next afternoon at their apartment on Bank Street. I had to stay up that night and print them. The next afternoon Rick came by and he took me with him to John and Yoko's. We were met by several assistants in the front room, rather like an office, and then we were ushered to a room in the back that turned out to be a big bedroom that was painted and furnished completely in white. It felt nothing like the usual over-the-desk business appointment. Though I was there because John and Yoko wanted to select a photograph for the album cover, we sat on their bed while I showed them the pictures.

While John and Yoko produced the Elephants' Memory album, a lot of people came around to the studio. The Elephants were a very popular and political band. They played at all the rallies and benefits. People from the artistic, radical, hippie leadership visited the studio—people like Jerry Rubin and Abbie Hoffman. Also David Peel, who was more of a W. C. Fields than a leader. Peel had this nonstop rap and he would say anything to anyone as long as they stood near him. He had a group of backup singers he dubbed The Lower East Side. One of the reasons these sessions (and later the rehearsals for the live show) grew confusing was that The Lower East Side was a dozen *different* people every day. All these people filled up the hallway outside the studio—loitered is the word, really.

John and Yoko were new in town and they enjoyed meeting everybody—though they became selective very quickly. Still, for a few months, the whole world dropped in. Mick Jagger was an old friend. Andy Warhol came by. Nureyev came in with Geraldo Rivera. Little entourages trailed in and out. One night the studio was subjected to a group from a college videotape commune. They set up a tripod in the hall. Mick Jagger came walking through and they asked him, "Could you be in our film?" He said yes, only he sat down right underneath the tripod so they couldn't get a shot of him except possibly the top of his head. Altogether, it was a very distracting way to work. But the Elephants were playing a very raucous kind of rock and roll music, so maintaining a raucous atmosphere in the studio made sense to John.

John and Yoko really enjoyed playing with the Elephants. Although they are a tough group of guys, the Elephants respected Yoko and appreciated her avant-garde style of music. When she started wailing, the sax player would start playing along, and the guitar player in particular was sensitive to her vocal styles. They wanted to try it live, and they agreed to appear at a benefit for the Willowbrook Foundation for Retarded Children. Rehearsals were held in a place called Butterfly Studio, which was a few blocks from where I lived.

Things were pretty convenient. I went to the studio regularly and every couple of days I developed and printed the pictures and took them around the corner to John and Yoko's apartment. That's how we developed a rapport: I'd go by, we'd have a cup of coffee and look at the pictures, have a neighborly chat.

I have a fond recollection of these rehearsals. Just a closed set of musicians rehearsing John Lennon's songs, a lot of which were Beatles songs to me. The band played straight-ahead rock and roll behind him. They worked out songs like "Imagine" and "Cold Turkey." The evening ran well into the early morning hours, with John and the band reviving old rock and roll songs: Chuck Berry, Bo Diddley, Little Richard, Eddie Cochran. John and Yoko knew I would be driving to within half a block of their house, so instead of calling for a car they had me drive them home after the sessions. I had a little black Volkswagen and they appreciated the anonymity of it.

While they were gearing up for the live concert there was a lot of hopeful talk about a tour. . . . Then they opened in Madison Square Garden, and it was one of the most exciting shows I'd ever seen. (I was standing behind a monitor five feet away from John when he sang "Imagine." *That* was unforgettable.) There were two drummers, two bass players, a wild unruly feeling onstage, and the audience was really rocking out. "Cold Turkey" was incredible. John was really singing it like he knew it. Then, for an encore, John turned around and called out, "Hound Dog!" and the band instantly rocked into it. During the second verse, John called on Stan Bronstein for the next solo, but Stan unclipped his sax, put it down, ran to the side of the stage, grabbed his girlfriend, and did a dance with her that was a showstopper. Later the band remembered that they had never rehearsed that song. . . . However, the reviews were less than encouraging. Some people suggested that they might have refined the show out of town first. Four days later John and Yoko played a Jerry Lewis telethon, but that was their last public performance together.

My wife, Nadya, came with me to the concert, and backstage she met Sara Segal, who was John and Yoko's assistant at the time. Sara had begun to feel the pressure of working for John and Yoko and she too wanted an assistant. The fact that we lived close by and that Nadya is intelligent made it easy for Yoko to hire her for the job. Within a couple of weeks, Sara decided to take a leave of absence. Nadya continued to work for John and Yoko on and off for the next few years.

At the time, I owned one of the only videotape machines in the neighborhood. John and Yoko were very familiar with video, but they didn't own one, so they came over to my house to watch tapes. The first time was after the Jerry Lewis Telethon on which they had appeared live. *Everybody* wanted to see it, so when I said, "Come on down to my house," they came—the band, John and Yoko, the crew, their friends—and we all watched the video together. I had other videos; they ranged from Muddy Waters to the New York Dolls. At four in the morning, after a dinner break, we all came back to my house to watch *more* videos. At one point there were a few Hell's Angels sharpening their knives in the kitchen; the Elephants' Memory guys were talking to some of the Ikettes sitting on the couch; and John and Yoko were sitting on the floor in the middle of this commotion, having a real heart-to-heart conversation. I remember standing in the living room with Nadya, surveying this extraordinary scene, and I turned to her and said, "Well, we've got quite a full house tonight."

After the Madison Square Garden concert, John and Yoko continued their relationship with the Elephants. The Elephants were involved with political activists of almost every stripe, but this was also the beginning of the feminist movement. In the sixties the credo had been "free love, free life, tune in, turn on, drop out." But it became evident that the credo was applied unilaterally, it was *men* talking, and women were still cast in the mold prepared by previous generations. John did not have a feminist background. He was a rock and roller who had a fairly chauvinistic way with women, particularly since as a Beatle he had had enormous numbers of women available to him. Elephants' Memory were not well grounded in feminism, either, but they all came from an artistic background and they were committed to progressive activity and a desire to comprehend and translate their feelings. Although they were macho men, they all had intelligent, enlightened mates—strong women who wouldn't sit by idly and be treated like dolls, and following Yoko's lead, they wanted more and more to be respected and taken seriously. Most of us eventually broke up with our wives. John was the only one lucky enough to grow and to get back with his mate and partner.

Together they made "Approximately Infinite Universe," Yoko's first record in America. In England she had made an album that was considered "experimental" music, and that's what her early reputation was based on—expressing feelings as sounds, which people didn't understand very well at all. With the Elephants she started constructing songs that were political and feminist statements. Yoko wrote a song called "Men Men Men," one of the first songs in which women talked about men the way men had so frequently talked about women—as playthings. The band couldn't easily relate to that. It was a brave thing for Yoko to record in this environment, backed by guys who were dressed in black leather and studs with all kinds of cowboy accessories, drinking at least six bottles of tequila between six people, and playing hard rock and roll behind her feminist ideas.

Sessions lasted pretty late. By the time Mick Jagger arrived on the scene, the sessions had been going on for a few weeks. There had been a lot of drinking because spending time in the studio gets boring. A simple guitar overdub can take hours. A musician would sit in the studio playing the same note over and over while John and Yoko and the engineer listened to that note over and over, and the rest of the band hung out in the other room smoking cigarettes. To pass the time, you end up talking about what you did in "show and tell" in the third grade. It's never really as exciting as it might sound. So I went home. I had just crawled into bed when the phone rang. It was Claude Hayn, the road manager for the Elephants. "You have to come back to the studio right away," he said. "Mick Jagger's on his way over." It was four-thirty in the morning when I got there. Sure enough, five minutes later Mick walked in. Present company consisted of just John and Yoko and the band. Wayne Gabriel of the Elephants is a great guitar player, and John wanted Mick Jagger to hear Wayne, so the three of them spent about an hour and a half jamming on the floor. The sounds of these men interacting inspired Yoko to write a song, and when they finished the jam, they all sat down at the piano and started singing Yoko's song and working out the arrangement, John and Yoko and Mick together ("I Have a Woman Inside My Soul").

That album marked a difficult period for John; absorbing all the feminist rhetoric and trying to deal with it in a perpetually drunken state caused a lot of turmoil. The situation became more and more intense. And *other* problems were building up. John and Yoko were suing ex-manager Allen Klein and vice versa, and their money was being held in escrow. Moreover, John and Yoko were under deportation order by the federal government. There were strong indications that their phone was tapped, and that the FBI was watching them. Nixon was up for reelection and Jerry Rubin invited everybody down to his house to watch the election returns. John and Yoko said they'd try to make it, but the album came first. When the session was over it was around four in the morning, the results were already in, and Nixon had won. In the studio we had drunk about eight bottles of tequila, but we still had six more in a shopping bag, so we drove down to Jerry Rubin's. It was quite an evening of drinking and screaming and ranting and raving. I remember in the car John was cursing with a vocabulary that would have been the envy of a Liverpool sailor. It's the only time I ever heard so many curse words in such a torrential flow. He was outrageously angry at everything. So he drank a lot, and that didn't help anything.

In the spring of 1973 my wife, Nadya, was working full time as John and Yoko's personal assistant. They were looking for a quieter place to live, so Nadya asked her mother to find a real-estate agent in Connecticut who might assist them. I drove John and Yoko up in their station wagon. To get the feel of Connecticut, we stopped at Nadya's mother's house, and they went for a walk in the backyard woods where I took some photos. All they wanted was to find a place where they could collect themselves for a while.

A press conference was called by John and Yoko to announce the creation of Nutopia, a borderless country John and Yoko had conceived that encompasses the entire world. According to their program, every citizen of Nutopia would be an ambassador for the country. The flag of Nutopia was the white flag of surrender. It was an expression of John's immigration predicament, and at the same time it reminded people that we are all human beings in the same world.

When Yoko was busy preparing material for her next album, *Feeling the Space,* I frequently visited their new apartment at the Dakota. This was her own project, and John wasn't involved. John and I would watch TV and drink tea. John didn't know very much about cooking. We sat in the kitchen at the Dakota and he offered to cook lunch—tea and toast. That was *cooking* for him. His other big meal was corn flakes and milk; he could "cook" that also.

John was very proud of Yoko, but occasionally during the making of her own record his jealousy flared up. He had a hard time dealing with the fact that his records hadn't sold well recently, coming as this did on top of his legal and financial problems. People still expected him to be a Beatle, but he didn't want that, though what he tried to do on his own didn't seem to be working. He loved Yoko, he liked what she did, and he was proud of her. And yet there *was* artistic jealousy. In fact, there was a video done of a piece Yoko wrote called "Winter Song," and I remember John saying, "It's so beautiful, I wish I could have written it myself." And he added, "I try to be understanding, and say to Yoko, 'Of course you can write and do what you want'—but most probably this song was written at six in the morning when 'the pig' was asleep, and she could finally be alone and create without pressure from me." He couldn't quite come to grips with it; she wanted to go on creating, and he was having trouble. . . . He was hard to live with at that time. He was a very frustrated, angry man, and to blow off some steam, he went to Los Angeles. It was the only time during their marriage they were separated.

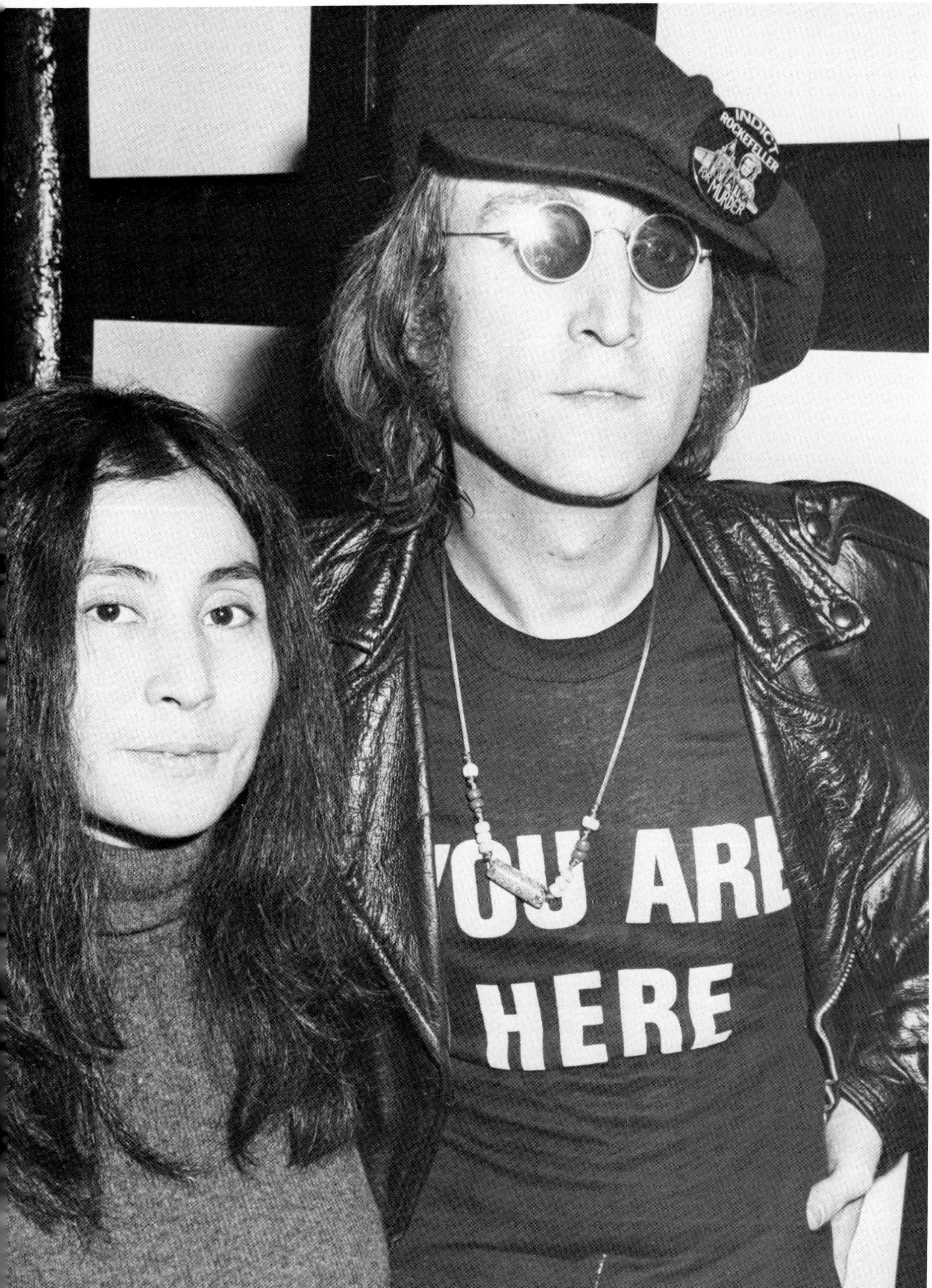
INDICT
ROCKEFELLER
FOR MURDER
OU ARE
HERE

23

30

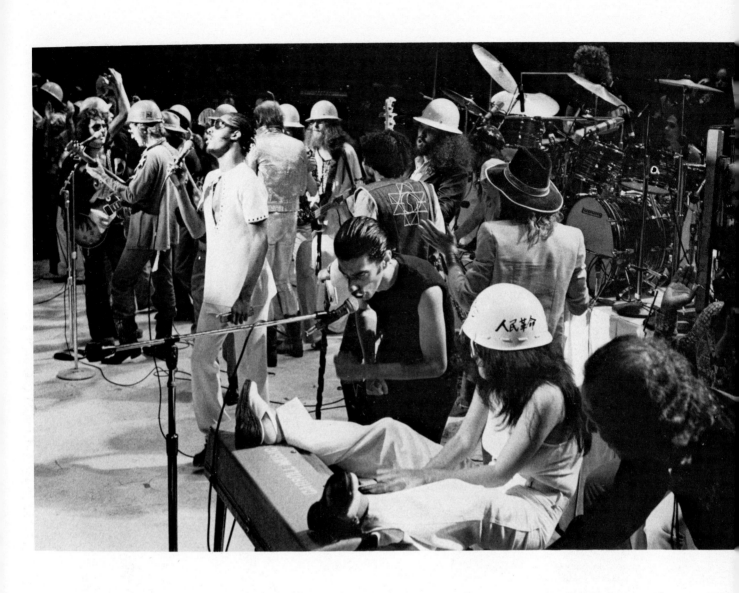

51

Part Two

In the summer of 1974 John returned to New York. I heard on the radio that he was going to be in Central Park for a March of Dimes Walkathon show sponsored by a local radio station. I got there just as his limo pulled up. When he got out of the car, I fell into step behind him. He went onstage, waved, and said, "Hi, I'm John Lennon," and the whole crowd started screaming. To keep him there a little longer, someone thrust a baby into his arms. On the way out John recognized me and casually said, "Oh, hi, Bob, how are you doing?" I hadn't seen him for at least half a year, during which time I wondered if I would ever see him again, if he would ever make it back from L.A., or if he'd move on to the Himalayas. But there he was, back in Central Park. "Come down to the studio to see us," he said.

John called Kenny Asher, Nicky Hopkins, Klaus Voorman, Jesse Ed Davis, and Jim Keltner for his next project, the *Walls and Bridges* album. Elton John came to one of the sessions, and they recorded "Whatever Gets You Through the Night." It was a pretty serious time. John had found that having forty people, stoned on whatever drugs they could carry, all playing and yelling at once wasn't the best way to make a record. He had wanted to capture the wild feeling of rock and roll but it had gotten out of hand. After trying it for the second time in L.A., he realized that wasn't the way to do it.

They wanted an album cover for *Walls and Bridges,* and the art director, Roy Kohara, suggested an idea that John thought was worth doing. They needed a series of head shots exactly the same size so they could cut them up and fit different expressions over each other, ending up with five differently composed faces. Using cardboard flaps that would overlap, they printed one face in the background and then another face on each flap, so you could compose John's face with a variety of noses and mouths. The art director wanted Avedon to do the photos. John respected that, but he didn't want to deal with yet another relationship and have to go to an unfamiliar studio. Since he was involved with me every day and trusted my work, John insisted that I do the session. I knew he didn't want to go anywhere, so I transported a makeshift studio to his house. I took ten rolls of him making faces and expressions.

The ad campaign was called "Listen to This . . ." and the basic ad was simply a picture of John's eyes. There was a "Listen to This Billboard," "Listen to This Press Kit," "Listen to This T-shirt," "Listen to This Matchbook," "Listen to This Cash Register," even "Listen to This Bus." We stood together on his roof, behind which was a dramatic skyline; it suggested a strong New York feeling. I said, "Do you still have that New York City T-shirt I gave you?" and he went in and put it on and came back with a dungaree jacket, and we took a set of pictures. It turned out to be one of the best-known sessions we ever did.

While we were taking pictures on the roof, John said, "Let's do a picture of me pointing to where I saw the flying saucer." He had told me the story once before. One night I had received a phone message, "Dr. Winston called." Winston was his middle name and his secret nickname. I called back and he said, "You gotta come over right away. I have some film for you to develop." He said he was sitting in his living room when he saw some blinking lights through the doorway. He didn't pay any attention to them at first because he thought it was a neon sign or maybe a balloon. He said he walked out onto the balcony and there he saw a flying saucer. Across the street there were some low buildings and then another tall building, and it was floating between his building and the tall one. He said it looked so much like the kind of flying saucer he'd seen in movies that he didn't think anything was strange. It was just floating slowly by, not making a sound.

An assistant who was there came running out onto the balcony and started taking pictures. John said that as the saucer started floating downtown he shouted to it: "Wait! Come back, come back! Take me with you!" but it floated away. Then he called me to develop the film; he was convinced he had pictures of it. I took it home and put the roll of film between two rolls of film I had taken and developed them. My two rolls of film came out perfectly, but his roll was blank. When I came back with the blank film I asked him, "Did you call the newspaper?" and he said, "I'm not going to call up the newspaper and say, 'This is John Lennon and I saw a flying saucer last night.' " So *I* called up the police and asked if anyone had reported a flying saucer. Their response was, "Where, up on the East Side? You're the third one." Then I called up *The Daily News*. They said, "On the East Side? Five people reported it." Finally, I called up *The New York Times* and asked them if anybody had reported a flying saucer, and they hung up on me.

To dramatize his impending deportation case, I wanted to create an image that would in some way support his defense. . . . I suggested that we take a photo by the Statue of Liberty. Around ten in the morning, I picked him up and we drove down to South Ferry and parked the car. As we walked around he surveyed all the buildings in the Wall Street area, and he said ruefully, "I bet I'm paying rent on every one of these buildings. There's a lawyer working on something for me in every one of them. You know, there's a funny thing about lawyers that work for us. The first time we go to visit them, they have a nice, respectable practice. By the time we go back for a second visit, they've moved to a bigger office, and it always has our picture on the wall."

En route to the Statue of Liberty, a group of about thirty schoolgirls coming off the ferry recognized John and they swarmed around him, clamoring for autographs. He calmed them down, and as quickly as he could he accommodated the group. It was ironic that here he was, about to be deported by the U.S. government, but the children didn't recognize whatever trumped-up threat he was supposed to represent. They just adored John Lennon.

In November, John was invited to the opening of *Sergeant Pepper's Lonely Hearts Club Band*, a musical play based on the Beatles record. He was thrilled that someone had written a play based on his music. At the reception following the show, two models invited us out for a drink. There had been a lot of people at the party, and many of them were getting drunk and loose. When we left the party, a throng of reporters followed John so he had me take the two models to my car. Then John left the party in his limo. He drove to the corner, jumped out of the limo, switched into my car, and we took off, thinking we'd eluded everybody. When we got to the girls' place, three

English reporters were waiting in the lobby. Somehow they had sussed it out. . . .

That night, John wasn't really a gentleman. We went upstairs and had a drink. John had been telling me all day about a Billy Swan song called "I Can Help," a rockabilly love song that goes, 'If you've got a problem, anything at all, if your child needs a daddy, I can help.' John went on about how he wanted to write a song like that. I hadn't heard it yet since it had just come out that day. He said, "But it's on every radio station," and he looked around and found a big radio one of the models owned and he was turning the dial, turning the dial, getting frustrated because he couldn't find the song. He picked up the radio and shouted, "Something's wrong with this radio," and then he threw it across the room and it smashed against the wall. The girl asked me, "Where do I send the bill?" and I said, "I don't know. *You* invited him." He wasn't always a good guy to drink with. I suggested to him that we leave. The reporters were still downstairs, but there was no story for them. It was one of the few times I saw John lose control. Thereafter I noticed a change in him. Although there were nights when he could be self-destructive, there were fewer and fewer of them. He was cleaning up his act and really seemed ready to enter a new phase of his life.

When John appeared at Madison Square Garden with Elton John, on Thanksgiving, 1974, I arrived in time to take pictures as he came onstage. He hadn't performed in a long time. Elton had asked him, after they recorded "Whatever Gets You Through the Night" together, "Will you come on tour and perform the song with me?" And John told him, "If it gets to be a number-one hit, I'll come and play it with you at the Garden." And it did become a number-one hit, so he honored his promise.

The next public appearance he made was at the Grammy Awards in February 1975. Both he and Yoko went. He was scheduled to present an award with Andy Williams and Paul Simon. David Bowie was also one of the presenters. That night wound up being a lot of fun, a relaxed confluence of the major pop stars of the moment. Bowie and Lennon were huddling close all night. That's where they got the idea to write the song "Fame," which they recorded over the next few days.

Around that time Yoko became pregnant. In the months before Sean was born, I saw them from time to time, twice a month maybe, which could be twice in one week and then not for a month and a half. I remember one day in particular. It was in late June or early July, a really hot, muggy New York day. I went to see John at the Dakota and he was sitting in the kitchen, having a cup of tea. I came in and stopped in my tracks. "Don't laugh," he said. He had shaved his head. I asked, "How does it feel?" and he said, "Great." And then I realized: I was looking at a *bald Beatle*. And yet I didn't think in terms of a photographer. I was a friend and he didn't want me to laugh, much less take a picture.

There was one night in June of 1975 when I moved out of one apartment and into the one where I now live. I hadn't seen John in a few weeks or so, and out of the blue he called and asked, "Can I come over?" and I said, "Sure, but I'm in a new apartment in the far corner of my building. It's hard to find. Just push the buzzer and I'll come down and get you." A half an hour later I began to wonder where he was, and I was about to go downstairs and wait for him when all of a sudden he came walking into the apartment. He said he'd had some fun in the building. I live in an artists' housing project and when he got lost and started knocking on doors asking for me, people recognized him and invited him in, saying, "I'm an artist, too. Look at my painting," or "Look at my sculpture," or "Let me cook dinner for you," or "Watch me dance." By the time he found my apartment he was exhausted. All he needed was to relax a little, and I made him some coffee. It wasn't exactly a momentous occasion, but considering that John Lennon was the first guest in my new home, it was an auspicious debut.

Part Three

I first saw Sean two months after he was born. They didn't have any baby pictures to send home to John's aunt. As a typical father, he wanted to send pictures home to the family. John and Yoko had taken snapshots themselves but he called me to take a set he could send out. We started in the living room, then John changed the baby's diaper, and we took some more photos in the master bedroom. John, Yoko, and Sean all wore kimonos, and John tied his hair in a ponytail so it would look neat. This was not the wisecracking pop star; this was the proud poppa. He seemed able to express more love and caring than ever before. He was happier that day than I'd ever seen him.

After the birth of Sean, John's life became more private. Yoko was amused and was enjoying motherhood, but John really wanted to do the work of caring for the baby. He knew about diapers and food and sleeping and *everything*. My cousin is a doctor who happened to be on duty in the hospital where Sean was born. He commented one time that John was the most attentive and involved father at the hospital. The hospital staff was surprised to see John show up for every single feeding. *He* wanted to hold the baby—not strangers. For John, that meant he had to wake up every four hours; but he was there every time, around the clock.

In the winter of 1976, John went into court against Morris Levy, the president of Roulette Records. Levy had received a demo tape while John was in the studio in 1974, and he released it through a TV offering. John sued them because it wasn't an authorized release. They went to the Supreme Court in downtown Manhattan. John had cut his hair, and he was wearing a suit and tie. Part of John's purpose there was to show Allen Klein that he wasn't afraid to go to court to straighten out his legal situations. They won their case, I might add.

Shortly after the court appearance, I called John and Yoko and was told, "No, we can't see anybody; we have a flu. Come back in a few days." Four days later I was told that they were going on a fast to cleanse their bodies. They wound up not eating solid food for forty days. After a few visits, I noticed that their thinking was altered by this regime, and the longer they fasted, the more perceptive they seemed to be about the world around them. Still, John's thoughts centered on food. He started to read cookbooks and books about nutrition. William Dufty's translation of Georges Ohsawa's book *You Are All Sanpaku* started him on a macrobiotic diet he continued from then on. He would read long and involved recipes, and he learned to prepare the healthy meals he was reading about. Nutrition became of utmost importance to him after that.

My son and I were asked to stay for dinner one evening after their fast had ended. John cooked for hours. He prepared a beautiful roast fish accompanied by rice and vegetables and it was delicious. Here was a guy who only three years earlier thought a meal was corn flakes and milk! I was genuinely impressed with the changes in his attitude and his serious commitment to a good life. Occasionally I'd call to see if he was interested in going to a show or a club, but he never felt like going out. Still he would tell me, "Keep calling. You never know when we will feel like going out." I called one time, and he whispered, "Hold on a sec," and he put the phone aside. I heard him playing guitar and softly singing a child's lullaby. Then he picked up the phone and in a hushed voice said, "I'm just putting the baby to sleep. What do you want?" . . . What could I say? He was in a peaceful and happy state of mind and I was content to let him preserve it.

In the fall of 1976, he was granted a green card, which gave him official permission to stay in the United States. That was the triumphant finish to a long fight. The conclusion of the deportation trial was an exciting day. A number of celebrities testified as character witnesses in his defense—actress Gloria Swanson, sculptor Isamu Noguchi, Norman Mailer. I was proud to have contributed the ID picture on his green card. There was no reason for him not to live here, and the court's decision was a bit of reaffirmation of humanity for him.

One by one, he and Yoko dealt with the obstacles. He got through the immigration hearing; then came the dissolution of their agreement with former manager Allen Klein. I was home asleep at four in the morning. John called up, and I answered the phone. "Bob?" he said. "This is John. Are you busy?" I said, "John, it's four in the morning. I can clear off my appointments." "We're settling with Allen Klein now. It's time to take a picture, so come to the Plaza Hotel and bring your cameras," he said. They had rented a full floor and a half in the Plaza Hotel and the suites were occupied with lawyers and their assistants. The largest suite had a huge conference table surrounded by lawyers and assistants—all representatives for Apple, Ringo, George, and Paul. John was the only ex-Beatle present. Yoko had been particularly active in the negotiations, talking to Klein's people, then talking to all the Beatle people, then talking to Klein's people, back and forth for a couple of *years*. When I arrived, the contract was almost settled. They hammered out an eighty-seven-page agreement, but some of the lawyers decided at the eleventh hour to change one paragraph and it had to be retyped. There was another room with secretaries and typewriters and two Xerox machines going full-blast at five in the morning, and they had already been there for days!

While they were retyping, Allen Klein went out and got breakfast for everybody. We were sitting around talking and John told me, "You know, when we signed the management deal with Allen Klein, it was a one-page contract with one paragraph on it." Then the moment came to sign the release. Klein had brought back a three-foot-long loaf of rye bread to put on the table and use as a prop so that when they put the contract on top of it, the photograph would look as though they had all agreed to "split the bread". . . .

Afterward we walked out into the dawn, and since I had just bought a brand new 1954 Buick, a classic rock and roll car, I volunteered to give them a ride home. John said, "Do we all jump in the front like a teenage movie?" On the way home, I told them that the singer of the Bay City Rollers said he'd love to meet John. John said, "Tell him if he's got a group in five years I'll meet him." I asked, "Well, is there any advice you could give him? Because I'm going to see the group tonight." "Tell him to get all the money he can in his own name *now*," was his succinct reply.

One day Yoko called me in the afternoon. "Bob, do you have a suit?" she asked. I said, "Yoko, I have a very nice suit from when I got married." She said, "We have an extra ticket tonight, so would you like to come to the ballet with us?" And she added, "And bring your camera to take some pictures." It was a performance by the Merce

85

Cunningham Dance Company—the avant-garde goes to Broadway—and therefore a special theatrical event. I was glad to go. John even wore a tuxedo. Following the show they went to a reception where they met celebrities from a variety of backgrounds. They sat with James Taylor and Carly Simon and with Merce Cunningham. Yoko was an old friend of his from the Fluxus art movement of the 1960s. She introduced him around to all the pop celebrities and everybody seemed to get on pretty well. But this was one of the few public appearances they made in this period.

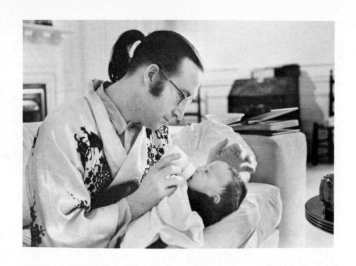

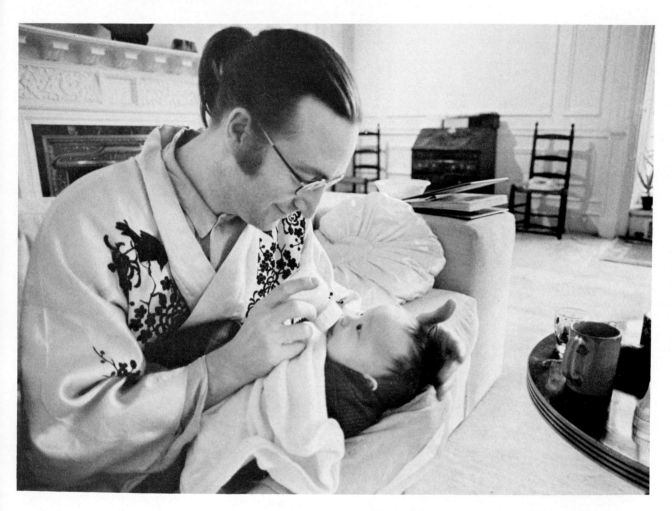

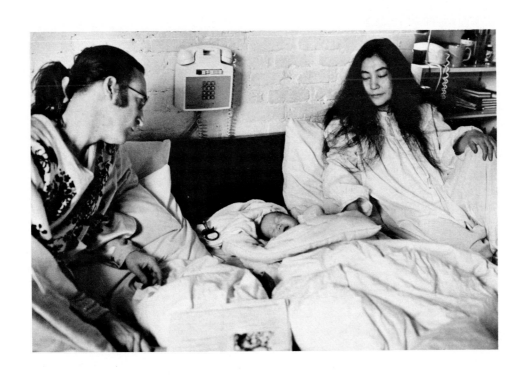

91

94

Part Four

In the summer of 1980, Yoko called one morning to say, "It's time to come to the studio tonight. Bring your cameras and we'll see you there." It was the last night of recording the basic tracks of the *Double Fantasy* album.

When I walked into the studio, I immediately noticed that John was leaner, firmer, and even from across the room I could see his physical transformation. He also seemed to be mentally clear about everything—his direction, his limitations—and he was celebrating his new attitude. And John and Yoko were so in touch with each other; producing the album they were like a tag team. They spent about half the time sitting on the same chair or holding each other. When the session ran into the late hours and they began the mixing process, Yoko would take a nap while John took control, and then when John needed a break, Yoko was at the helm. John referred to Yoko as Mother. He kept saying, "Well, what do you think about that, Mother?" If they were doing one of Yoko's songs and somebody said, "John, what about the bass line?" he would say, "Ask Mother." Very affectionately, without sarcasm.

The next morning I went to the Dakota at noon. Yoko and John came walking in about two minutes later. John was lively and full of energy. Yoko excused herself saying, "Look, I have some business calls to make. You boys go have some coffee and I'll meet you at the recording studio later." John and I went to a coffee shop on Seventy-first Street, ordered espresso, and had a long talk.

He told me about a trip around the world he had taken not long after he and Yoko got back together. He had traveled by himself. It was one of the few times in the past fifteen years that he had ventured out of the house alone. He said he took only a little bag and caught a flight to Hong Kong. He went there first because it was distant, remote, and they wouldn't recognize *John Lennon of the Beatles*. It was the first time in his adult life he could walk down the street and not be recognized. He reached the hotel by himself, and he managed to negotiate a room without any assistance. When he closed the door to the room, he found he was shaking. He was so excited about just being a person, not a celebrity surrounded by paid help and sycophants. He was in the room and he wanted a cup of tea. He knew how to call room service but he had *never* done that. He never had to. Things people take for granted were first-time experiences to him. Even when he was a teenager, he was already in rock bands, and very early on they had lots of fans who did everything for them, to the point that when he was a Beatle anyplace he went, strangers would do anything for him. He removed himself from all that when he went to Hong Kong. He vividly recalled standing in the room with his cup of tea, looking out the window in the early morning, watching people streaming down the street. He walked out of his hotel and followed the flow. He took a ferryboat across the harbor along with a group of Chinese workers, feeling safe and anonymous. He said it was the biggest weight off his shoulders. He could be just another person in the world.

He also told me a story about a boat ride he took from Bermuda. Among the things he took up as a rich househusband was sailing, and he hired a captain and two crew members to run his boat and teach him how to sail. They went to Bermuda where they discovered a boat for rent called *Imagine*, a huge, oceangoing sailboat. He chartered it for a voyage back to his house on Long Island. They embarked under a sunny, clear sky and perfect sailing conditions. He described being out at sea as being in the middle of nowhere. "You are the only thing in the universe," he told me. "The entire place is blue; like two blue disks, one is above you and one is below you, and there's nothing else except you, this little dot, and that is your entire world."

That's where they were when the storm came up. The crew and the captain became ill, to the point where they had to stay on their beds, unable to function at all. John described the sight of twenty to thirty foot waves crashing over the bow. You have to keep the bow pointed into the waves, he explained, because if you go sideways and a wave comes, the boat will capsize. And this happens no matter how much money you have. He resented the fact that here he was, the multimillionaire dilettante on a luxury cruise, and all of a sudden it was up to *him* to save not only his life but the others' as well, *because he was the only one who could stand up* (which he felt was due to his macrobiotic diet). The idea was to hold the wheel steady while plowing into the waves. It's a matter of physical endurance. He said they had to tie him to the wheel because the waves were so high he might otherwise wash off the deck.

They gave him a yellow jacket and a hat. "You're dressed up like a sailor, so you can say, 'Today I am a sailor,' " he told me. He remembered someone telling him you're supposed to sing sea chanties to get into the rhythm of turning the wheel. "All I knew were Beatle songs," he said. So he sang a medley while the storm raged. He said it was the most exciting thing he'd done since the Beatles played Shea Stadium. . . .

In the next few weeks, while they made *Double Fantasy*, John was in a distinctly positive mood and was expressing optimism for the future. He felt that paying attention to his well-being had renewed his inspiration, and his relationship with Yoko had reached a higher ground. Raising Sean made him appreciate life more than ever. He was full of confidence and was planning a world concert tour.

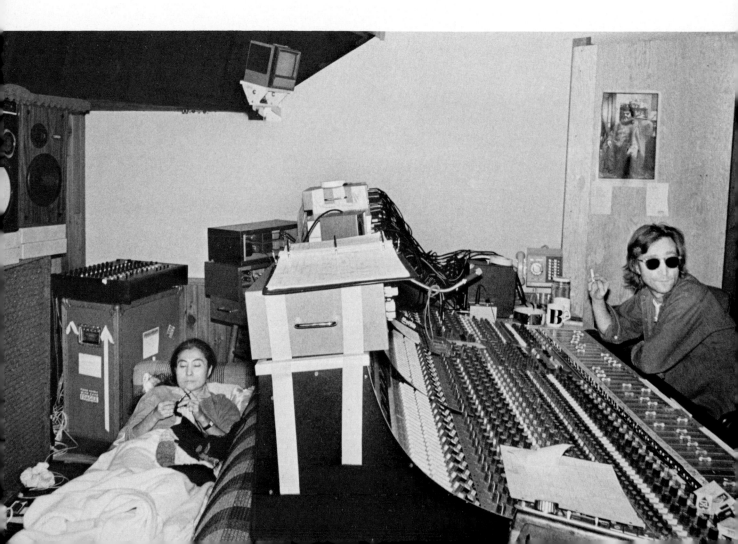

In December, following the release of the "Double Fantasy" album, *The Village Voice* asked for some photos to illustrate an article they were running about John and Yoko. I called Yoko and she said, "Come by the studio. I'd like you to hear what we're doing." At the Record Plant they were mixing a new dance single by Yoko called "Walking on Thin Ice." We sat in the control room for a while. Yoko was resting on the couch, and John and I sat on the floor and talked about things like his early days at the Star Club in contrast to the current scene. He felt proud to have been part of the Beatles, but I remember somebody saying to him, "Why don't you unite the Beatles?" and he answered, "Why don't you go back to high school? You go on in life," he said. "You don't go back."

Finally we were leaving about eight-thirty or nine in the morning, and on the way out I said, "Did you want to take some pictures?" Yoko was tired, but John said to her, "Come on, you kept him up all night." I took a photo of them on the sidewalk, with the sun coming up behind them. As they got into the car, John turned and said, "We'll see you later."

Index